Sadness

CAUSES & EFFECTS OF EMOTIONS

Embarrassment, Shame, and Guilt

Happiness

Fear and Anxiety

Romantic Attraction

Anger

Optimism and Self-Confidence

Stress and Tension

Sadness

Empathy and Compassion

Envy and Jealousy

Surprise and Flexibility

Emotional Self-Awareness

Loneliness

CAUSES & EFFECTS OF EMOTIONS

Sadness

Z.B. Hill

Mason Crest

Mason Crest
450 Parkway Drive, Suite D
Broomall, PA 19008
www.masoncrest.com

Printed and bound in the United States of America.

First printing
9 8 7 6 5 4 3 2 1

Series ISBN: 978-1-4222-3067-1
ISBN: 978-1-4222-3078-7
ebook ISBN: 978-1-4222-8771-2

Library of Congress Cataloging-in-Publication Data

Hill, Z. B.
  Sadness / Z.B. Hill.
     pages cm. — (Causes & effects of emotions)
  Audience: Grade 7 to 8.
    ISBN 978-1-4222-3078-7 (hardback) — ISBN 978-1-4222-3067-1 (series) — ISBN 978-1-4222-8771-2 (ebook) 1. Sadness—Juvenile literature. I. Title.
  BF575.S23H55 2014
  152.4—dc23
                                                        2014004384

CONTENTS

KEY ICONS TO LOOK FOR:

Text-Dependent Questions: These questions send the reader back to the text for more careful attention to the evidence presented there.

Words to Understand: These words with their easy-to-understand definitions will increase the reader's understanding of the text, while building vocabulary skills.

Series Glossary of Key Terms: This back-of-the book glossary contains terminology used throughout this series. Words found here increase the reader's ability to read and comprehend higher-level books and articles in this field.

Research Projects: Readers are pointed toward areas of further inquiry connected to each chapter. Suggestions are provided for projects that encourage deeper research and analysis.

Sidebars: This boxed material within the main text allows readers to build knowledge, gain insights, explore possibilities, and broaden their perspectives by weaving together additional information to provide realistic and holistic perspectives.

INTRODUCTION

The journey of self-discovery for young adults can be a passage that includes times of introspection as well joyful experiences. It can also be a complicated route filled with confusing road signs and hazards along the way. The choices teens make will have lifelong impacts. From early romantic relationships to complex feelings of anxiousness, loneliness, and compassion, this series of books is designed specifically for young adults, tackling many of the challenges facing them as they navigate the social and emotional world around and within them. Each chapter explores the social emotional pitfalls and triumphs of young adults, using stories in which readers will see themselves reflected.

Adolescents encounter compound issues today in home, school, and community. Many young adults may feel ill equipped to identify and manage the broad range of emotions they experience as their minds and bodies change and grow. They face many adult problems without the knowledge and tools needed to find satisfactory solutions. Where do they fit in? Why are they afraid? Do others feel as lonely and lost as they do? How do they handle the emotions that can engulf them when a friend betrays them or they fail to make the grade? These are all important questions that young adults may face. Young adults need guidance to pilot their way through changing feelings that are influenced by peers, family relationships, and an ever-changing world. They need to know that they share common strengths and pressures with their peers. Realizing they are not alone with their questions can help them develop important attributes of resilience and hope.

The books in this series skillfully capture young people's everyday, real-life emotional journeys and provides practical and meaningful information that can offer hope to all who read them.

It covers topics that teens may be hesitant to discuss with others, giving them a context for their own feelings and relationships. It is an essential tool to help young adults understand themselves and their place in the world around them—and a valuable asset for teachers and counselors working to help young people become healthy, confident, and compassionate members of our society.

Cindy Croft, M.A.Ed
Director of the Center for Inclusive Child Care at Concordia University

Words to Understand

perceive: See, hear, or sense something.

evolved: Changed over a very long time.

species: A certain kind of life form that is capable of breeding to produce new life forms of the same type.

survival mechanisms: Ways that life forms have evolved to survive in their environment.

distract: Take your attention away from what you're supposed to be doing.

community: The group of people you live with or nearby or with whom you share something in common, such as religion or ethnic background.

psychologists: Experts on the human mind and emotions.

symptoms: Signs that you have a disease. For example, a fever is a common symptom of the flu.

insomnia: Not being able to sleep.

ONE

WHAT IS SADNESS?

Imagine the following situations:

- Your dog dies.
- Your best friend moves to the other side of the country.
- Your favorite shirt is ruined.
- You lose a piece of jewelry you've worn for years.
- Your house burns down.
- You fail your driver's test.
- Your boyfriend or girlfriend breaks up with you.
- You lose your new phone.

How do you feel in each of these situations? You may feel a combination of things—frustration, disappointment, helplessness, and anger are a few possibilities—but chances are your main emotions in each of these situations is sadness.

Each of us feels many different emotions every day. Often, we feel more than one emotion at once.

Sadness is the emotion we feel when we've lost something. It could be a big loss—your dog's death, for example—or a small loss—your favorite shirt. We feel sad when things aren't going the way we want them to. We usually think of sadness as the opposite of happiness. It's one of the main negative emotions human beings experience.

WHAT ARE EMOTIONS?

Emotions are our inner personal experiences in reaction to the world. People used to think that emotions took place in the heart. They thought "heart" feelings were very different from body feelings. Today, however, scientists believe that what we *perceive* as emotions are really changes in our bodies, especially changes in our brains. Different kinds of situations in our lives trigger different responses inside us. We've learned to give all these responses labels—like "happiness," "sadness," "anger," and "fear." Many experts think that people actually feel only six main emotions—happiness, surprise, fear, sadness, disgust, and anger—and that all the other emotions we experience are some sort of combination or variation of these six.

You've been feeling emotions your entire life, ever since you were a baby. You probably can't imagine what life would be like without them. Your emotions do an important job. They direct your attention toward things that are important. When something makes you sad, for example, your emotions say, "Notice this! This isn't a good situation! Try to change this situation!" Or when something scares you, your emotions tell you, "Be careful!" Your emotions make a bridge between the outside world and the actions you need to take. They help you know what to do next. Ever since you were a young child, you've been learning from your emotions: what makes you happy and what makes you sad, what scares you and what makes you laugh. Then you've learned to adjust your behavior accordingly.

Scientists today believe that humans **evolved** to have emotions because these inner feelings helped us survive in a dangerous world. Early humans' brains were triggered by something in the outside world—a source of food, for example, or a possible mate or a dangerous animal—and then a rush of brain chemicals made your long-long-ago ancestors feel things that prompted them to act in various ways that helped them survive. Those behaviors included smiling, shouting, fighting, making friends, and falling in love. In one way or another, all these things helped humans survive as a **species**. Being happy or sad, angry or surprised, compassionate or jealous were all **survival mechanisms**.

TYPES OF SADNESS

Like most emotions, sadness comes in many shades and flavors. The sadness you feel when you lose a favorite earring is very different from the sadness you feel if a grandparent dies.

Feeling discouraged after losing a game or getting a bad grade is completely normal. It's what you do next that matters most—trying again to succeed or giving up.

We use language to help us sort out the various ways we feel this emotion. Here are some of the words used to describe different types of sadness.

- **Agony:** This word describes a very powerful sadness or pain.

- **Anguish:** Similar to agony, anguish is an intense emotional pain.

- **Dejection:** Feeling dejected means you feel crushed emotionally. You may experience this feeling when you are not being accepted or appreciated.

- **Discouragement:** This describes the feelings that go along with failure. After you've tried something and failed, especially if you've tried and failed several times, you may feel as though you'll never be able to succeed. You want to give up. Your self-confidence has gone down.

- **Dismay:** Dismay is a form of sadness that often occurs when something unexpected happens. It can include feelings of shock and disappointment.

- **Distraught**: Someone who is distraught is very upset. She may scream, sob, or be out of control in some other way.

- **Distress:** This can describe any sort of uncomfortable emotional experience. It can include anxiety and sadness.

- **Grief:** Grief is a deep, powerful feeling of sadness that comes after a major loss in life, such as after someone has died.

14

SADNESS

Feeling sad when you miss your friends or family is entirely normal, even in a world where we're all so connected by technology. Being away from the people you care about can be hard even if they are just a text or call away.

- **Homesickness:** This is a feeling of sadness that comes from being away from the place where you feel most comfortable. You may experience homesickness because you miss your friends and family, but you may also feel this way simply because you long for familiar surroundings.

- **Hurt:** Hurt is what you feel after you have been wronged in some way, usually by someone you love or trust. You feel betrayed.

- **Regret:** Regret is often what you feel after you have made a mistake. You feel sorry for what you have done. Regret may also be much like disappointment.

- **Sorrow:** Sorrow often goes along with feelings of regret. You may feel sorrow after hurting another person, losing an opportunity, or when the outcome of something is not what you were hoping for.

- **Unhappiness:** This word describes a general sense of sadness, a "blue" or gloomy feeling. It may not be pinned to any specific loss, and it may vary in how strong it feels.

Make Connections

Many people seem to feel happier when the sun is shining and sadder on gray, gloomy days. Some people, though, actually become depressed during the winter months when there's less sunshine. This is known as seasonal affective disorder (SAD). About 1 to 2 percent of the population has this problem. It's especially common among women and young people. To fight SAD, doctors suggest exercise and getting outside as much as you can. Exposing yourself to bright artificial light may also help.

SADNESS

Depression is a mental illness, not simply a deep sadness. While we all feel sad from time to time, not everyone experiences depression.

SADNESS AND EVOLUTION

So if emotions started out as simply survival mechanisms, how did sadness do anything to help our ancient ancestors live? It might not be obvious what good a feeling like sadness would do for people facing endless dangers, from animals that wanted to eat them to neighboring tribes who fought with them over food supplies. You would think that sadness would just **distract** them from all the other things they needed to do to survive!

Scientists, however, think that sadness does in fact have survival benefits. When people are sad, their brains focus on what went wrong. They slow down and think. They may take a step back from life for a period of time. This can help them avoid dangers and similar losses in the future. It gives them a chance to take a look at their lives and see what's working and what isn't. They have time to recover so that they can then get on with life.

Humans also express their emotions on the outside. Early humans learned to recognize what sadness looked like in each other. Tears and frowns and slumped shoulders all signaled to friends and family that someone was feeling sad. They knew that something was wrong. Then they could take action to help the sad individual. This action from the **community** in response to sadness was also a survival mechanism. It helped humans survive, even in the midst of a world full of danger and loss.

Sadness tells us that something is not going well in our lives. It gives us an opportunity to take a look at our lives. It can help us grow. Too much sadness, however, can get in the way of living our lives. It can even make us sick.

WHEN SADNESS BECOMES DEPRESSION

Sadness is something everyone experiences. It's a normal human emotion. Sadness is what we feel when something hurts us in some way. Little sadnesses and big sadnesses will come our way often during our everyday lives. Sadness comes and goes.

Research Project

Find out more about the connections between weather and moods. Use the Internet and the library to find out if there are scientific reasons why people feel sadder during certain kinds of weather. Then do a survey of at least 20 people (friends, family, other students, teachers). Find out how many people feel that their emotions are affected by the weather. Report your findings.

When sadness doesn't go away, though, it may be an emotional illness **psychologists** call depression. Depression is more than a temporary mood. Psychologists list these **symptoms** of depression:

- a "down" mood that doesn't go away
- lack of pleasure in all or most activities
- significant weight loss or weight gain
- *insomnia*
- feeling tired most of the time or a loss of energy
- feeling worthless
- not being able to think or concentrate
- thinking about death or suicide

People who have these symptoms for more than a few weeks may need help. Depression can be a dangerous illness. It can

Make Connections

Each year, nearly 19 million adults are diagnosed with depression.

Text-Dependent Questions

1. What are the six main emotions experts believe all people experience?

2. Explain the role that evolution played in human emotions.

3. The text says that sadness was a human "survival mechanism." Explain what this means, according to this chapter.

4. Explain how depression is different from sadness.

5. What is seasonal affective disorder?

make people not take care of themselves the way they should. It can cause them to miss out on important life experiences. Sometimes it can even lead to death. So if you or someone you know is depressed, it's very important to get help.

A mental illness like depression can be triggered by life events, like a death or some other big loss. But the reason it doesn't go away is because the cells inside a person's brain aren't working normally. Scientists have linked both depression and normal sadness—and all emotions—to chemical reactions inside our brains.

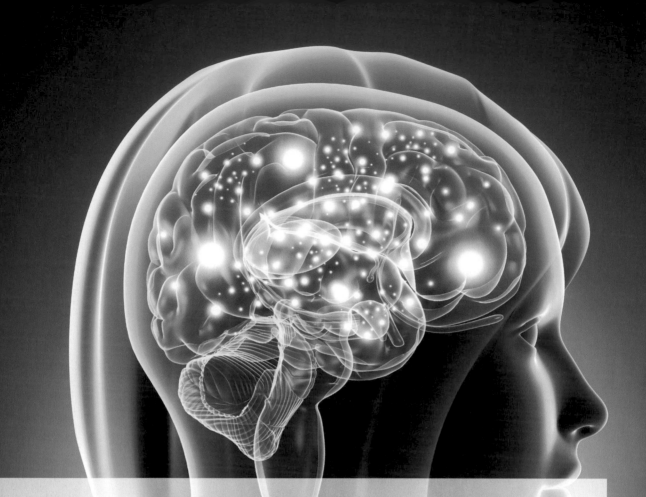

Words to Understand

regulate: Control.

researchers: Scientists who look for answers to questions and make new discoveries.

receptors: The parts of your nerve cells to which neurotransmitters can attach.

sophisticated: Complicated, very developed and advanced

technology: Tools or processes that humans invent.

vulnerable: Likely to get hurt or sick.

heredity: The process of passing something from one generation to the next.

chronic: A sickness or condition that lasts for a long time.

ulcers: Painful holes in the lining of your stomach.

acid reflux: When acid from your stomach comes back up toward your throat.

TWO

WHAT'S THE CONNECTION TO YOUR BRAIN & BODY?

We often talk as though emotions spring from our hearts. We talk about our hearts breaking; we say, "I love you with all my heart." We say things like, "My brain tells me one thing, but my heart tells me something different." When we talk like this, we probably don't really mean that we think the organ in our chests that pumps our blood is what gives us our emotions. We may not be exactly sure what we *do* mean. Scientists, though, tell us that our emotions are actually produced inside our brains.

THE BRAIN AND SADNESS

Certain areas of the brain **regulate** our moods. **Researchers** believe that the connections between nerve cells and the chemicals

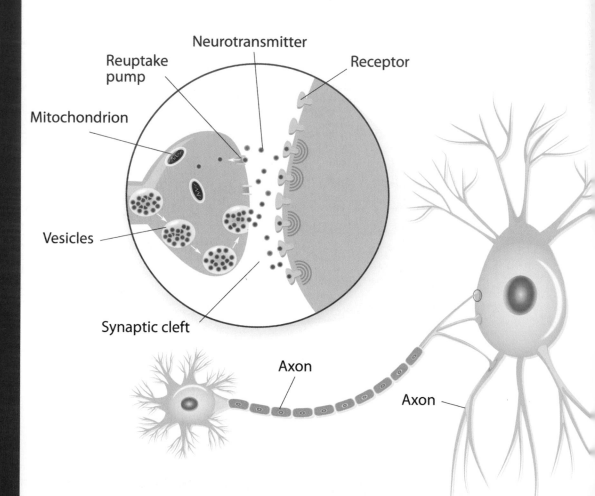

Neurotransmitter

Reuptake
pump

Receptor

Mitochondrion

Vesicles

Synaptic cleft

Axon

Axon

This diagram shows the way in which neurons send signals along their axons
and release neurotransmitter chemicals to bind to receptor sites on the second
neuron.

Make Connections

Here's how neurons communicate:
An electrical signal travels down the axon, which is the long part of the nerve cell.
Neurotransmitter chemicals are released.
The neurotransmitter binds to receptor sites on the neuron.
The signal is picked up by the second neuron and is passed along.

within our brains all play a role in sadness. Each neuron (nerve cell) has a tiny gap between it and the next neuron. This gap is called a synapse. Special chemicals called neurotransmitters carry messages across the synapse.

This network of neurons is very complicated, and scientists still aren't exactly sure how everything works. Researchers have new ways of looking inside the brain, however, which are helping them learn more every year. Positron emission topography (PET), single-photon emission computed tomography (SPECT), and magnetic resonance imaging (MRI) are all ways of looking inside the human body. An MRI scan can track changes that take place when a region of the brain responds during various tasks. A PET or SPECT scan can map the brain by measuring how many neurotransmitter **receptors** are in certain areas.

Using this **sophisticated** imaging **technology**, scientists now know that three areas of the brain play large roles in sadness—the amygdalae, the thalamus, and the hippocampus.

The amygdalae are part of the limbic system, a group of structures deep in the brain. Emotions such as anger, pleasure, sorrow, and fear are all triggered by reactions within the amygdalae. Researchers have found that nerve cell activity is greater within the amygdalae whenever a person is sad.

The thalamus receives information from the senses, and then relays it to the cerebral cortex. The cortex is the part of your brain

LIMBIC SYSTEM STRUCTURES

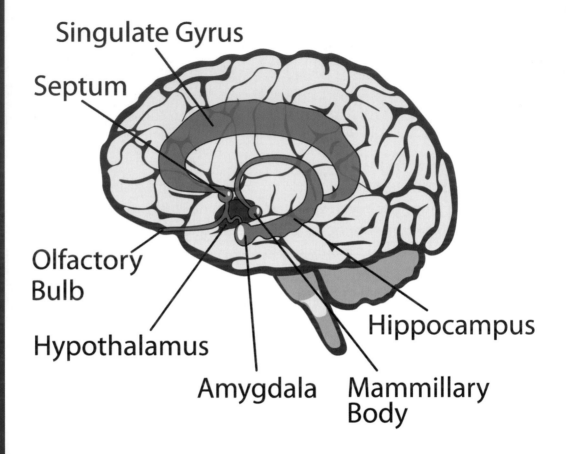

Singulate Gyrus

Septum

Olfactory
Bulb

Hypothalamus

Amygdala

Mammillary
Body

Hippocampus

The limbic system is responsible for the emotions we feel, the things we remember, and the way we act, among other functions.

that directs high-level functions such as speech, movement, thinking, and learning. The thalamus is what links your perception of events in the outside world with the feelings we label as sadness.

The hippocampus is another part of the limbic system. It has a central role in processing long-term memories. This is the part of your brain that registers fear when you are confronted by a

Make Connections

Scientists have identified many different neurotransmitters. Here are a few that play a role in sadness and depression:

- Acetylcholine helps us remember. It is involved in learning and recall.
- Serotonin helps regulate sleep, appetite, and mood, and it keeps us from feeling pain too badly. Researchers have found that some depressed people have lower levels of serotonin.
- Norepinephrine makes blood vessels become more narrow, raising blood pressure. It may trigger anxiety and be involved in some types of depression. It also helps provide us with good feelings that act as rewards to motivate us to act—so if we don't have enough of this neurotransmitter, we may feel as though we don't care about anything.
- Dopamine is essential to movement, but it also influences motivation and plays a role in how a person perceives reality. Problems in dopamine transmission have been associated with psychosis, a severe form of distorted thinking where people may have hallucinations or delusions. It's also involved in the brain's reward system. People who abuse drugs may have problems with their dopamine levels, which can contribute to depression.
- Gamma-aminobutyric acid (GABA) is a chemical that researchers believe helps calm anxiety.

particular danger—and then warns you of that danger the next time you run into it. Researchers have found that the hippocampus is smaller in some depressed people. They believe that the chemicals released by sadness may keep nerve cells in this part of the brain from growing normally. After a person has been sad or

While scientists aren't sure if sadness and depression are entirely hereditary, they are sure that there is some connection, and that a depressed parent might create an environment that breeds depression in the children in the house.

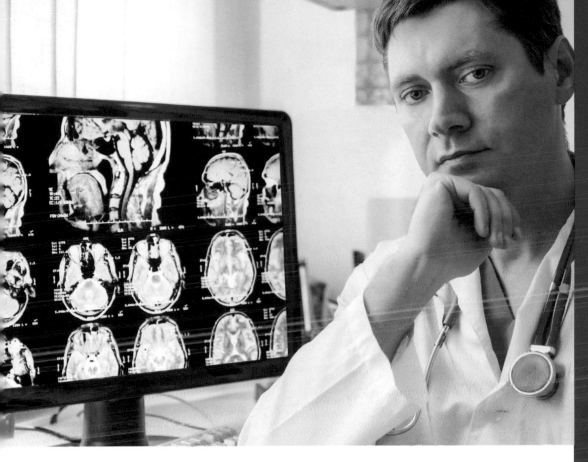

Using MRI scans of the brain, doctors have discovered the places in the brain from which our emotions come, but there are many discoveries left to make about the way our brains interact with our emotions.

depressed for a long time, it takes a while for her brain to return to normal. Scientists believe that's because nerve cells in the hippocampus have to regrow.

SADNESS AND GENES

Inside each one of your cells are long strands of DNA that carry your genes—the instructions passed on to you from your parents, which determine what you're like in many different ways. The color of your hair, whether you're male or female, and your intelligence

Make Connections

Scientists have found these connections between genes and moods:

- Studies of identical twins—who share the same genes—show that if one twin has a mood disorder, the other twin has a 60 to 80 percent chance of developing a mood disorder too.
- If a person has someone in her immediate family—a parent, brother, or sister—who has gone through a major depression, she has a 3 percent greater chance of going through depression as well.

are just some of the instructions that are carried from generation to generation. Scientists have discovered that genes also play a role in emotions.

It's not simple, though. Just because your mother tends to be sad a lot, for example, doesn't necessarily mean you will be too. Dozens of different genes affect mood. Even then, even if you do carry genes that make you more likely to be sad and depressed, it doesn't mean you'll definitely be depressed. Your environment—what's going on around you—also plays an important role. Researchers think that certain genes make some people more **vulnerable** to depression when they run into hard times, while other people with different genetic makeups may more easily get through the same emotional challenges. Researchers are working hard to find out more about the connections between mood and **heredity**.

SADNESS AND THE REST OF YOUR BODY

Sadness starts with changes in your brain—but it doesn't stop there. Sadness and depression can also cause these health problems.

Research Project

This chapter explains the way brain chemicals play a role in our moods. When people cannot regulate their moods, their brains are not working correctly. This was once called "being insane" or "going crazy," but doctors now talk about mental illness instead. Using the library and the Internet, find out more about the role that brain chemicals play in mental illness. Explain the connections between neurotransmitters, emotions, and three different mental disorders, including bipolar disorder, schizophrenia, and depression.

• *Digestive system problems:* Sadness can make your stomach ache. This is especially true for children and adolescents. Nausea and diarrhea can go along with depression, and *chronic* digestive problems, like *ulcers* and *acid reflux* disorders, can be made worse by depression.

• *Headaches:* Many things can cause headaches, but sadness is one of those things. Headaches that are related to depression usually feel dull; your entire head may hurt, rather than any specific area of your head. People with depression often say their headaches are worse in the morning and in the evening.

• *Muscle aches:* If you're depressed, you may feel as though you hurt all over. This may be caused partly because you're not moving around enough and partly because you're tensing up your muscles.

• *Chest pain:* A pain in your chest could be a sign of a heart attack or other serious heart condition, but in young people, it's more often caused by feelings of sadness and anxiety. You may feel as though your heart is pounding or fluttery, and it may be

SADNESS

Sadness and depression can lead to health problems, from a headache to serious stomach issues.

Text-Dependent Questions

1. Explain what neurotransmitters do.

2. List five different neurotransmitters and explain one thing that each does.

3. What are three kinds of imaging technology described in this chapter that allow researchers to look inside the human brain?

4. According to this chapter, what three brain structures are involved in sadness?

5. How are genes connected to sadness and depression?

6. What are four ways sadness can affect the rest of your body?

difficult to breathe. Make sure you talk to your doctor if you experience this.

Sadness and depression are powerful emotions. They can make you physically sick—and they can also change your life in other ways.

Words to Understand

creativity: The ability to make new things.

inspire: Create a feeling or idea in a person.

stress: When your body and mind are under pressure.

introspective: Having to do with thinking about your own thoughts and feelings.

destructive: Having to do with something that hurts your life.

coping mechanisms: Things that help you deal with a hard part of your life.

defensive: Having to do with protecting yourself.

THREE

How Can Sadness Change Your Life?

Five-year-old Lacey loves her goldfish. She spends hours watching it swim in its tank. She likes feeding it and seeing it gulp down the bits of food. One day, though, when she looks at the fish tank, she sees that her goldfish is floating upside down. It's not moving anymore. Her goldfish is dead. Lacey bursts into tears. For the rest of the day, she cries whenever she thinks of her goldfish. She is very sad.

Most of us had an experience a little like Lacey's when we were young. Since then, we've probably gone through many other kinds of losses. We've been sad many times.

Lacey says to her mom, "I wish I'd never had a goldfish. Then I wouldn't feel so sad."

Most of us have felt like this too. We realize that if we'd never had something we valued, then we wouldn't have had to go through the pain of losing it.

SADNESS

Sometimes, our most painful moments, memories, and feelings inspire our most creative expressions, even if being creative in a crisis can be difficult.

Make Connections

Have you ever noticed that sometimes people like to read sad books and watch sad movies? It's almost as though we love to be sad. A recent study done at Ohio State University found that the reason people love sad stories so much is that they actually feel happier after watching or reading something sad. Dr. Silvia Knoblock-Westerwick, the lead author of the study, explained: "Positive emotions are generally a signal that everything is fine, you don't have to worry, you don't have to think about issues in your life. Negative emotions, like sadness, make you think more critically about your situation. So seeing a tragic movie about star-crossed lovers may make you sad, but that will cause you to think more about your own close relationships and appreciate them more."

Eventually, though, most of us—including Lacey—will realize that sadness is just one of the ways we appreciate the things in life we value most. We learn to treasure our memories. Lacey may draw pictures of her goldfish. She may make of stories about it. Maybe she'll decide she wants to learn more about fish and how to take care of them, so that next time she has a fish she can help it to live longer. Sadness often spurs our **creativity**. It can **inspire** us to find solutions to problems.

If we were never happy, then we would never be sad either. Sadness helps us appreciate the good things in our lives. Researchers tell us that periods of sadness give us time to evaluate our lives, to think more deeply.

In the end, sadness is simply a part of being human. It's a part of how we're made. Sometimes it can change our lives for the better—and sometimes it cause us more problems on top of the sadness.

SADNESS

Sleeping more than usual can be a sign of depression. Sometimes, depression can keep you up at night, making you sleepy the next day.

SADNESS AND SLEEP

Sadness can get in the way of your normal sleep patterns. You may find it hard to fall asleep at night—or you may wake up in the night and not be able to get back to sleep.

Sleep problems can then make you more tired during the day. When you're tired, your brain's chemicals get thrown out of whack. This can make you feel even sadder! Even though it may be hard to fall asleep, getting enough sleep is one of the best things you can do for yourself when you're sad. Sleep can help your brain recover and get back to normal.

If weeks go by, though, and you start noticing that you're still sleeping more than usual, this could be a symptom of depression. Depression—sadness that doesn't go away—can also make you want to sleep more than you usually do. If you're depressed, you need to get help from a doctor or a counselor.

SADNESS AND EATING

When you're sad, the changes in your brain can send signals to your stomach to shut down for a while. This can mean that you lose your appetite.

On the other hand, the **stress** that often goes along with sadness might make your brain send out signals that you need *more* food. Your body thinks it's getting ready for a crisis where you'll need all the nutrition you can get. Some people may gain weight because they eat more when they're sad.

Good nutrition is important, all the time. A healthy, balanced diet will help keep your brain working at its best, which will help keep your emotions stable and balanced. So it's important to eat something even if you don't feel hungry when you're sad.

If you notice that that there's been a change in your appetite—whether you're eating more or less than usual—that lasts more than a week or two, this could be another sign that you're depressed. If you think you're depressed, ask for help!

SADNESS

Escaping from negative feelings by eating may work for a short period of time, but, eventually, we have to face the way we feel without snack food or other unhealthy distractions.

SADNESS AND JUDGMENT

Have you ever heard someone use the phrase "sadder but wiser"? These words imply that feeling sad can actually help us to know and understand the world better. Researchers have discovered that there's actually some truth to this.

Happy people don't usually spend as much time thinking. They don't examine their lives or themselves. They may not notice their own faults. Sad people, however, become more **introspective**. They think about what they've done wrong. They focus on ways they can change. They try to think of things they can do make their life better. Their sadness can help them grow into wiser, more thoughtful people.

But sadness can work the other way too. Sad people may blame themselves for things that went wrong. They may lose confidence in themselves. Their self-images may suffer. This is particularly true of people who are depressed. Sadness can be creative—but depression is often **destructive**. Depressed people can't think clearly. They're seldom able to work creatively. They often feel stuck in a rut.

SADNESS AND THE FUTURE

When people are sad, they have various **coping mechanisms**. One person might eat more. Another might want to take lots of hot baths. Someone else might like to listen to music to cheer himself up, and still another person might go for long walks alone. Everyone deals with sadness in different ways.

Researchers have noticed one thing, however, that many sad people have in common: they're less likely to want to wait for things. They're not very patient. They want things NOW.

A recent study found that sad people spend more money. They're less willing to save for the future. They want to enjoy their money right now! The people in the study were even willing to give up larger sums of money that they would get in the future in favor of smaller sums they could spend right now. The sad people

Often, sadness and anger are closely linked. You may get angry at the people you love because you're sad or hide your sadness by getting angry.

were also willing to spend more money for something they wanted than non-sad people were.

If you find yourself feeling sad, you should probably try to avoid making decisions about money that could affect your future. In your sad mood, you could short-change your future self in order to get something right now. Sadness won't last forever—so put off making decisions like this until your mood changes. Don't decide to empty out your college fund after your girlfriend breaks up with you. And don't blow all your savings on a new wardrobe just because you're feeling down in the dumps.

SADNESS AND OTHER EMOTIONS

Sadness can also get tangled up with other negative emotions. These emotions may come before or after our sad feelings. Sometimes, it's really hard to sort through what we actually feel about a certain situation! Here are some of the possible emotions that you might find mixed in with sadness:

- *Anger:* Anger is how we often respond to situations that threaten us in some way. It's a *defensive* response to an uncomfortable situation. We may feel angry when people fail to live up to our expectations or when something seems unfair. Sometimes we would rather feel angry than feel sad, so we mask our sadness with anger.

- *Blame:* Blame is when you decide another individual caused the situation that's making you sad. It's that person's fault. You feel wronged.

- *Stress:* Stress is a physical reaction to some sort of life challenge. When we're stressed, we may feel overwhelmed. Scientists tell us that stress is part of the fight-or-flight response. When humans—and all other animals as well—run into something that could be a threat to them, their bodies respond by getting them ready for whatever comes next.

Sadness or depression can make little things seem overwhelming. You may have more trouble concentrating on schoolwork or staying awake in class.

Make Connections

Here are some ways to tell if you might be depressed:

1. Do you have a hard time making even small decisions, like what to do on a Saturday or what to wear in the morning?

2. Do you have a hard time falling asleep—or do you fall asleep and then wake up in the night and lay there for hours?

3. Do you have a hard time focusing on your schoolwork?

4. Do you find yourself eating either more or less than you usually do?

5. Do you feel more tired than usual in the morning?

6. When you think of the future do you feel discouraged by all the things you have to deal with?

7. Do you cry often?

8. Do you feel bored and lack energy to do things during your free time?

9. Do you have a lot of headaches and stomachaches?

10. Do you find yourself losing your temper over little things?

Everyone will answer "yes" to some of these things, but if you answer "yes" to 5 or more of these questions, tell an adult—your parents, a counselor, or a doctor. You may be experiencing depression—and if you are, you should get help!

Make Connections

 People who are depressed may think about suicide. They feel as though their sadness will never go away. They believe that death is the only way to escape. They may have thoughts like these:

- I can't stop the pain.
- I can't think clearly.
- I can't make decisions.
- I can't see any way out.
- I can't sleep, eat, or work.
- I can't make the sadness go away.
- I can't see the possibility of change.
- I can't see myself as being worthwhile.
- I can't get someone's attention.
- I can't seem to get control.

These thoughts are lies. No bad feelings last forever! Good times AL-WAYS return, sooner or later, if you just wait long enough. Even when you have been sad for a very long time, one day you will feel better. If you find yourself thinking these things—or if you know someone who says these things—get help!

A whole bunch of physical reactions happen, like the heart beating faster and the muscles tensing, all of which are designed to give the body what it needs for an extra burst of energy to either fight or run away. These reactions are normal and healthy—but they can add up. Sadness can cause stress, and stress reactions can then drain your energy and make you tired.

Text-Dependent Questions

1. What does this chapter indicate is the connection between sadness and creativity?

2. Explain why people may enjoy sad stories, according to researcher Silvia Knoblock-Westerwick.

3. According to this chapter, how can sadness affect your judgment?

4. How might sadness impact the way a person spends money?

5. Based on the sidebar that gives ways to tell if you're depressed, what are 10 possible symptoms of depression?

- ***Guilt:*** If you have wronged another person, you may feel guilt. You feel at fault. Sometimes guilt can trigger sadness.

- ***Anxiety:*** Anxiety is an emotion that's made up of feelings of nervousness, restlessness, and fear. Unlike fear, however, anxiety may not be connected to anything real. Instead, it's just a free-floating feeling. Like depression, anxiety is often caused by abnormal levels of brain chemicals. Anxiety and depression often go together.

SADNESS AND DEPRESSION

Sadness is normal. It comes and goes. Some losses are bigger than others, so it makes sense that the sadness they cause may take longer to heal—but with time, even big sadness fades away.

Depression isn't just a deep sadness; depression is an illness that needs attention from an expert. Just because it isn't a broken bone or a case of the sniffles doesn't mean you should ignore depression.

Research Project

This chapter says that good nutrition is an important way to keep your brain healthy. Use the library and Internet to find out what food groups are most important to the brain's health. Explain how specific foods support healthy brain function. Are there any food deficiencies that could cause mood disorders?

But sometimes, sadness turns into depression—and that's a different story. Sadness is something you have to accept as being part of your life. Depression isn't. Depression means you need to get help.

Words to Understand

values: Things that are important to someone.
humiliated: Feeling foolish or embarrassed.
justified: Having a good reason to be a certain way.
strategies: Techniques; ways of doing something.

FOUR

WHAT CAN YOU LEARN FROM SADNESS?

When Eva's brother died, her whole life changed. "I had been kind of a party animal until then," she reported. "All I cared about was having a good time. I thought life was just about having fun. I didn't really have any goals for the future. But after Ryan died, all the things that seemed like so much fun just weren't fun at all anymore. I spent a lot of time by myself, crying. I guess I just turned inward for most of an entire year. It was a really hard time in my life, a really painful time—but eventually, I guess you could say I started to heal. I still missed Ryan, but I'd wake up in the morning, and I didn't feel sad. Things made me laugh again. But I wasn't the same person I'd been before he died. I was more serious. During that year, I'd started painting pictures that expressed how I felt, and that was when I realized I wanted to be an artist. I decided to go to college and study art. Now, I kind of feel like my art is a gift that Ryan gave me. He helped me become someone I might not have been if I hadn't spent that sad year pulling back from my friends and what I thought were good times."

Brook went through a different kind of sadness when her father and her mother got divorced. "I blamed myself," she told a counselor. "For a long time, I felt as though it must have been my fault that Dad moved out. I started acting out, getting in trouble. But then both my parents spent a lot of time talking to me, doing stuff with me. They made it clear to me that they really loved me, that it wasn't my fault after all. After a while, I started seeing myself differently. They helped me see all the things about me that they loved, things I'd never thought about before. I still wish they could be together, that we could be a family again—but in a way, we're stronger than we were before the divorce. I feel like I understand myself better. I can see the good things about me that I never knew were there."

Levi was sad when his best friend moved away last summer. "Diego and I have been friends since kindergarten," he said. "We'd been together so long that he felt like a member of my family. I spent as much time at his house as I did at my own. We were always hanging out, but at the same time, I'd get really bugged by him. He had all these little habits that just got on my nerves. I wasn't always very nice to him. I kind of just took for granted that he'd always be there. And then suddenly, he wasn't there anymore. I was really sad. I really, really missed him. I realized how much I like him, how much we have in common. We started e-mailing each other, talking about all sorts of things we never even mentioned when we were seeing each other every day. It's a funny thing, but it's almost like we got closer after he moved away. I know we'll be friends forever."

THE MEANING OF SADNESS

Sadness isn't fun. No one likes to feel sad. But sadness has a purpose. Eva, Brook, and Levi all learned something as result of being sad. They grew. They learned to understand themselves and others better. In Eva's case, sadness made her slow down and become more introspective; her sadness helped her become more creative, while it gave her a new set of **values**. Brook's sad feelings made her parents pay attention to her in new ways—and when they did, they were able to help Brook build a strong sense of her own value. Levi's sadness made him appreciate his friend Diego in a new way, and he was able to build a stronger friendship because of that appreciation.

Sadness reminds us that something has been lost—and it pushes us to think about that loss. It makes us pay attention to what's really important in our lives. Sometimes, it also signals to others around us that we need help. It's still a difficult and painful emotion—but if we handle sadness right, it can actually improve our lives in the end.

Here are some questions to ask yourself the next time you feel sad:

- What have I lost? (It could be someone you love—but it might also be something physical, like a bicycle or a favorite piece of clothing; it might be your sense of your own importance or your reputation; it might be your health; it might be your trust in another person.)

- How important was this thing to me—and why?

- Does this loss hurt my sense of my self in some way? Do I feel **humiliated** or embarrassed? Have I been treated unfairly—or did I do something to deserve this?

- Do I feel powerless? Do I feel as though I have no control over my life?

- Do I feel frightened as well as sad? Are my fears **justified**? Has someone threatened me or injured me, either emotionally or physically?

Sharing your feelings with others is often a great way to make yourself feel less alone with your sadness. If you are facing depression, however, you may consider seeing a professional who can speak with you about your feelings.

- Have I lost something I had hoped to have in the future? Has a goal been taken away from me?

- Has a relationship been damaged? Was I to blame—or was there nothing I could have done to prevent this?

- How big is this loss? What impact will it actually have on my life?

- What can I do to recover from this loss? What will make me feel better?

- Do I feel guilty thinking about going on after this loss? Can I let go of my guilt? Can I be open to what the future holds?

- Do I need to get help? Is this loss too big for me to deal with by myself?

There's no single, right answer to any of these questions. Each situation is different, and each person's reactions will be different as well. But thinking about the answers to these questions will help you make sense of your sadness. It well help you understand your feelings better, so that you can learn from them.

SADNESS DOESN'T MEAN THAT LIFE ISN'T WORTH LIVING!

When we feel sad, we may feel as though the entire world looks gray. Nothing seems very interesting. Everything seems ugly and painful and difficult.

Sadness, however, is a reaction that takes place inside us. It tells us more about our inner world than it does the world around us. Sadness is how we respond to some circumstances. When we're in the midst of sad feelings, we feel bad—but the bad

Breakups can lead to sadness and sometimes to depression for many people. There are many negative ways to cope with a breakup, but remember that there are many positive ways to deal with painful emotions as well.

feelings won't last forever. If we hold on long enough, sooner or later life will start to seem interesting once more. Things will make us happy again. Actually, life probably won't have changed that much—but we will have.

COPING WITH SADNESS

Sometimes people try different ways of handling the losses that come along. They don't want to feel sad, so they do various other things instead.

Imagine your boyfriend has just broken up with you. You don't want to admit how sad you are, so instead, you try these coping mechanisms:

- ***You devalue the relationship.*** In other words, you tell yourself that your relationship with your boyfriend wasn't all that valuable to you after all. You never really liked him all that much, you say. You're better off without him.

- ***You memorialize the relationship.*** This means you refuse to let go of your memories of your times together. You spend lots of time looking at photos of the two of you together. You read his e-mail messages over and over.

- ***You substitute a new relationship in place of the old relationship.*** You go out and get a new boyfriend immediately!

- ***You deny that the breakup is real.*** You tell yourself that your boyfriend will come back to you. You refuse to admit that the breakup is permanent.

- ***You blame someone else for the breakup.*** You could blame your parents or your friends. You might even blame your boyfriend for being too stupid to realize what a good thing the two of you had together. You focus on your anger with whomever you feel is to blame—and that way you don't have to acknowledge what you may have done to contribute to the breakup.

- **You try to bargain.** Maybe you ask your boyfriend to give your relationship one more chance. You tell him if he'll go out with you again, you'll do something for him.

Sometimes these **strategies** may work. Or they may work for a while. Maybe you and your boyfriend will get back together.

But eventually, we all run into losses we can't bargain our way out of; we can't deny that they're real; we can't devalue them and convince ourselves they don't matter. We have to accept that we have lost something real. Something we cared about has come to end. It's not coming back.

As much as it hurts, life will go on after this loss. Now we have to decide what we want to do next. What path will we choose to lead us into a new future, a future that doesn't include that thing we lost?

Some strategies for moving forward are healthy and creative, while some aren't. Here are some options you might want to consider the next time you're sad:

- **If you want to eat or drink to deal with your sadness,** try exercising more instead. Food and alcohol can trigger the feel-good chemicals in your brain, but so does physical exercise. Going for a brisk walk, a bicycle ride, or a swim makes our brains release serotonin and dopamine, two of the neurotransmitters that help lift our moods. Overeating and alcohol may make you feel better in the short run, but in the long run, they can make you feel worse, both physically and emotionally. Exercise, however, makes you feel better both right now and in the future. It helps you cope with your sad feelings, and keeps sadness from turning into depression.

Make Connections

In the book *The Once and Future King*, author T. H. White offers this advice for dealing with sadness:

The best thing for being sad . . . is to learn something. That's the only thing that never fails. You may grow old and trembling in your anatomies, you may lie awake at night listening to the disorder of your veins, you may miss your only love, you may see the world about you devastated by evil lunatics, or know your honour trampled in the sewers of baser minds. There is only one thing for it then — to learn. Learn why the world wags and what wags it. That is the only thing which the mind can never exhaust, never alienate, never be tortured by, never fear or distrust, and never dream of regretting. Learning is the only thing for you. Look what a lot of things there are to learn.

- **If you take out your sadness on those around you,** instead, find other ways to channel your frustration with life. Take a karate class; write your feelings in a journal; or play something loud and sad on a musical instrument. Talking about your feelings to a friend can help too, but try not to talk to someone who will just encourage you to stay upset. You want friends who will listen and support you, while at the same time encouraging you to find new ways to think about your situation.

- **If you find yourself spending all your time working—either on your schoolwork or at a job—so you don't have time to think about your sadness,** consider getting involved with some kind of after-school

Research Project

This chapter offers three quotes from authors, each of which has to do with sadness. Read a fiction book that focuses on sadness in some form. Here are some suggestions:

Where the Red Fern Grows by Wilson Rawls
Bridge to Terabithia by Katherine Paterson
The Giver by Lois Lowry
The Red Pony by John Steinbeck

What role does sadness play in the story you choose? What loss has the main character experienced? How does the character cope with sadness? What does the character learn from it? How is the character changed by the end of the story?

volunteer work instead. Serve dinner at a soup kitchen for homeless people, walk the dogs at an animal shelter, or visit old people in a nursing home. By keeping busy, you'll keep yourself from brooding over your sadness—but at the same time, you'll feel the sense of reward that comes from helping others. That alone can lift your spirits. Also, as you become more aware of others' problems, your own may not seem as overwhelming.

- **If you find yourself tempted to go for "retail therapy,"** instead of heading to the mall, think about gifts you might buy for others. Make a scrapbook for your little sister, cook your mother's favorite meal, surprise a friend with a gift for no special occasion. Try to focus on others instead of yourself.

Text-Dependent Questions

1. Based on the stories given in this chapter, explain three ways that sadness might actually improve our lives.

2. Explain the coping mechanisms for dealing with sadness listed in this chapter. How might each be good—and how might each be a less than healthy way to cope with sadness?

3. Explain how, according to this chapter, exercise can lift your mood?

4. Explain how "retail therapy" connects with sadness. Use information provided both in this chapter and in chapter 3.

• **_If you feel like being alone,_** give yourself plenty of quiet time—but don't shut yourself off completely from your friends and family. Remember, sad times are opportunities for withdrawing and thinking—but they're also times for letting others reach out to us. You may find that you build stronger bonds with friends and family as a result.

Sadness is painful. But as author Jonathan Safran Foer reminds us: "You cannot protect yourself from sadness without protecting yourself from happiness." And Dr. Seuss, the beloved author of so many children's books, says: "Don't just cry because it's over. Smile because it happened." Sadness may have something important to teach you.

Find Out More

IN BOOKS

Franzen, Lenore. *Sadness*. Mankato, Minn.: Creative Co, 2004.

Hamil, Sara. *My Feeling Better Workbook*. Oakland, Calif.: Instant Help, 2008.

Monague, Mathilde. *Trouble in My Head: A Young Girl's Fight with Depression*. New York: Ebury, 2011.

Schab, Lisa. *Beyond the Blues*. Oakland, Calif.: Instant Help, 2008.

Van Dijk, Sheri. *Don't Let Your Emotions Run Your Life*. Oakland, Calif.: Instant Help, 2011.

ONLINE

Causes of Sadness in Teens
everydaylife.globalpost.com/causes-sadness-teens-13790.html

Depression
kidshealth.org/teen/your_mind/mental_health/depression.html

Depression Symptoms
www.medicinenet.com/depression/article.htm

Understanding Depression
health.howstuffworks.com/mental-health/depression/facts/understanding-depression-ga.htm

Series Glossary of Key Terms

adrenaline: An important body chemical that helps prepare your body for danger. Too much adrenaline can also cause stress and anxiety.

amygdala: An almond-shaped area within the brain where the flight-or-flight response takes place.

autonomic nervous system: The part of your nervous system that works without your conscious control, regulating body functions such as heartbeat, breathing, and digestion.

cognitive: Having to do with thinking and conscious mental activities.

cortex: The area of your brain where rational thinking takes place.

dopamine: A brain chemical that gives pleasure as a reward for certain activities.

endorphins: Brain chemicals that create feelings of happiness.

fight-or-flight response: Your brain's reaction to danger, which sends out messages to the rest of the body, getting it ready to either run away or fight.

hippocampus: Part of the brain's limbic system that plays an important role in memory.

hypothalamus: The brain structure that gets messages out to your body's autonomic nervous system, preparing it to face danger.

limbic system: The part of the brain where emotions are processed.

neurons: Nerve cells found in the brain, spinal cord, and throughout the body.

neurotransmitters: Chemicals that carry messages across the tiny gaps between nerve cells.

serotonin: A neurotransmitter that plays a role in happiness and depression.

stress: This feeling that life is just too much to handle can be triggered by anything that poses a threat to our well-being, including emotions, external events, and physical illnesses.

Index

About the Author & Consultant

Z.B. Hill is an author, actor, and publicist living in Binghamton, New York. He has a special interest in adolescent education.

Cindy Croft is director of the Center for Inclusive Child Care at Concordia University, St. Paul, Minnesota where she also serves as faculty in the College of Education. She is field faculty at the University of Minnesota Center for Early Education and Development program and teaches for the Minnesota on-line Eager To Learn program. She has her M.A. in education with early childhood emphasis. She has authored *The Six Keys: Strategies for Promoting Children's Mental Health in Early Childhood Programs* and co-authored *Children and Challenging Behavior: Making Inclusion Work* with Deborah Hewitt. She has worked in the early childhood field for the past twenty years.

Picture Credits

Dreamstime.com:
8: Michal Bednarek
10: 0katherina0celestial0
12: Jstudio
14: Monkey Business Images
16: Yupiramos Group
20: Shubhangi Kene
22: Designua
24: Nn555
26: Monkey Business Images
27: Andrei Malov
30: Piotr Marcinski
32: Ekaterina Staats
34: Odua
36: Milan Ljubisavljevic
38: Lasse Kristensen
40: Anita Patterson Peppers
42: Pavalache Stelian
46: Convisum
48: Dreamstime.com Agency
52: Elena Rostunova
54: Andriy Petrenko